INCREASING YOUR SOCIAL MEDIA INFLUENCE ON FACEBOOK.

Increasing Your Social Media Influence on Facebook.

Series "Social Media Influence"
By: Aaron Cockman
Version 1.1 ~November 2021
Published by Sherry Lee at KDP
Copyright ©2021 by Sherry Lee. All rights reserved.

No part of this publication may be reproduced, distributed or transmitted in any form or by any means including photocopying, recording or other electronic or mechanical methods or by any information storage or retrieval system without the prior written permission of the publishers, except in the case of very brief quotations embodied in critical reviews and certain other noncommercial uses permitted by copyright law.

All rights reserved, including the right of reproduction in whole or in part in any form.

All information in this book has been carefully researched and checked for factual accuracy. However, the author and publisher make no warranty, express or implied, that the information contained herein is appropriate for every individual, situation, or purpose and assume no responsibility for errors or omissions.

The reader assumes the risk and full responsibility for all actions. The author will not be held responsible for any loss or damage, whether consequential, incidental, special, or otherwise, that may result from the information presented in this book.

All images are free for use or purchased from stock photo sites or royalty-free for commercial use. I have relied on my own observations as well as many different sources for this book, and I have done my best to check facts and give credit where it is due. In the event that any material is used without proper permission, please contact me so that the oversight can be corrected.

Although the publisher and the author have made every effort to ensure that the information in this book was correct at press time and while this publication is designed to provide accurate information in regard to the subject matter covered, the publisher and the author assume no responsibility for errors, inaccuracies, omissions, or any other inconsistencies herein and hereby disclaim any liability to any party for any loss, damage, or disruption caused by errors or omissions, whether such errors or omissions result from negligence, accident, or any other cause.

This publication is meant as a source of valuable information for the reader, however it is not meant as a substitute for direct expert assistance. If such level of assistance is required, the services of a competent professional should be sought.

Contents

Introduction..6

Chapter no.1..8

Social media influence..8

What are social media influencers?........................9

Types of social media influencers include:..........9

Impact of social media...11

What is Facebook?..11

Chapter no.2..14

Choose the right social platform..........................14

Facebook...14

Analyze your competitors.......................................16

Chapter no.3..20

A Positive Influence on Facebook........................20

Top 10 Ways to Influence Facebook....................23

Chapter no...32

How to Grow Your Facebook Presence...............32

The Right Way to Grow Your Facebook Presence..........32

How to grow Facebook following in 2022:........39

9 essential steps...39

Chapter no.5..50

Successful Facebook Influencer...........................50

How to use Facebook analytics to assess.........61

the success of your approach...............................61

Chapter no.6...64

Use Facebook's Influencer..64

Marketing to Your Advantage...64

How Does Facebook Influencer Marketing Work?.........65

Finding Influencers on Facebook......................................66

Ideas for Influencer Marketing on Facebook...................68

Chapter no.7...71

Ideas for Facebook Influencer Marketing......................71

1. Promoting Giveaway Contests....................................71

2. Using Facebook Ads to Expand the Audience...........72

for Influencer Campaigns...72

3. Sharing Experiences through Facebook Live.............73

4. Cross-Promoting Campaign from Other Platforms...75

5. Standing Up for a Cause..76

6. Telling Stories Using Videos..76

Ready to Get Started with Facebook..............................78

Influencer Marketing?..78

How to Find Facebook Influencers.................................79

Conclusion:..85

Introduction.

Social media has all changed people's interactions, how businesses do business, and how ad expenditures are spent. As social media platforms grew in popularity in the previous decade, Facebook Inc. (FB) rocketed to the top of the heap, outpacing rivals Twitter Inc. (TWTR) and LinkedIn Corporation in terms of users and revenue. As of January 24, 2022, Facebook's market cap was $781 billion, with more than 2.74 billion active monthly users and mobile advertising accounting for 98.5 percent of the company's total income in 2019. When compared to LinkedIn (250 million MAU) and Twitter (100 million MAU), Facebook has a competitive advantage due to its enormous quantity of monthly active users (MAU) (330 million MAU). Facebook is the most popular destination for users to make shopping choices when compared to other social media networks, according to a recent poll from The Manifest, business news, and how-to website. Even though anti-Facebook sentiment, such as the #DeleteFacebook movement, continues to gather traction, this tendency persists. Consumers are more likely to buy from a brand they follow on Facebook (52%) than they are on Instagram, YouTube, Pinterest, Twitter, LinkedIn, Snapchat, and Reddit combined (48 percent).

According to some digital marketing experts, it is due to Facebook's standing as the world's largest social network and its targeting algorithm. "Facebook is a legacy social media network that many generations utilize," said Andrew Clark, a marketing strategist at Duckpin, a digital marketing business. "The formatting of posts undoubtedly attracts individuals with a higher intent to purchase because it tends to contain long-form content." Thanks to social media, people and businesses can communicate more efficiently, developing genuine customer connections. As a result, 67% of individuals have purchased after viewing a social media advertisement. "People feel connected to a business on social media, and they trust a brand," said Scott Levy, CEO of Fuel Online, an SEO and digital marketing firm. "The main point is to bring value to people, not to utilize social media as a selling platform." By producing commercials and interacting with influencers, brands may build a solid social media presence. It may aid in raising brand recognition and attracting new customers.

    People use social media today to interact with different brands differently, and they expect brands to reciprocate. While social media may be effective marketing and sales tool, it can also be essential to provide high-quality customer service and retain customers. Most customers connect with brands on social media by liking their postings (51%), which does not need a response. However, replying to people who leave reviews (31%), mention businesses on their profiles (22%), direct message brands (20%), and tweet at brands (18%) may result in loyal customers. "Social media acts as a marketing tool. It also serves as a customer service tool," said Melissa Orozco, CEO of the New York City-based Yulu Public Relations agency. While social media is an essential customer service and marketing tool, experts advise firms to consider the platform they choose and their target demographic when developing a social media strategy.

Chapter no.1

Social media influence.

Social media influence is a marketing phrase representing an individual's ability to influence other people's thinking in an online social community. The greater a person's influence, the more appealing to companies or other individuals looking to promote an idea or sell a product. Companies may use social media influence to boost brand awareness, inventory sales, and consumer engagement. It can be accomplished by executing a marketing plan that focuses on expanding its social media impact or recruiting well-known, reliable influencers in the field.

Measuring social media influence.

Influence can be measured at the most basic level by looking at the size of a person's social networks, such as LinkedIn connections, Twitter followers, or Facebook friends. However, determining how a person forms social connections, who those relationships are, and the amount of trust between the individual and their connections requires a more extensive investigation. Some experts recommend that social influence assessment methods be used. Klout is one such tool, which assigns a numerical score to an individual based on their online behavior on major social networking sites. On the other hand, other industry professionals have expressed reservations about the accuracy of Klout's measures, pointing out that Klout does not track all sorts of online activity. A blog piece from a reputable author, for example, could reach a limited but carefully targeted audience and hence be more influential than a simple tweet sent to thousands of people.

What are social media influencers?

A user who has built a reputation in a specific business or content type and has access to a large audience is a social media influencer. An influencer should have a large enough audience and enough authority to start a conversation and motivate people to take some action or change their behavior. Companies can engage social media influencers to help them grow their social media following, become more relatable, and support products and services.

Types of social media influencers include:

- **Celebrity influencers:** These are the most well-known influencers, as their celebrity status has given them a large following. Various celebrities attract particular demographics and target audiences. Companies that want to reach specific demographics and target audiences might engage a celebrity influencer to promote or endorse their product to their supporters.
- **Consumer influencers:** These are ordinary people who have earned popularity due to their personality and relatability. They are usually active on social media by publishing text, blogging, or sharing photos. Because their audience finds them "genuine" or "relatable," they are more likely to listen to their advice, such as when they recommend a service.

- **Micro-influencers:** also known as expert influencers, are ordinary people who have developed a following and topical authority due to their expertise in a particular field. When they praise or recommend a product, their target market is more inclined to trust them.
- **Professional bloggers:** vloggers and photographers are examples of content creators. Their responsibilities include creating new content that people will want to read regularly. Sending merchandise to a content creator as part of a company's marketing strategy could hope that they will evaluate and promote the product to their followers. Writing sponsored pieces for their site is another alternative.

Companies should think about a few things before hiring an influencer. The first is whether the influencer's message is compatible with the company's and relevant to the same target market. The second factor is how engaged the influencer is with their audience. Also, how trustworthy that comes across to their audience. Finally, evaluate the influencer's reach or several followers, as this might aid in predicting return on investment (ROI).

Impact of social media.

Social media is only going to become stronger as a communication and entertainment medium. Therefore, social platforms are only going to get stronger as their memberships rise. As a consequence, the following impacts of social media on society are apparent:

- Increasing awareness of social, ethical, environmental, and political viewpoints and issues.
- Quickly and effectively disseminating teaching materials
- Creating new marketing options for businesses.
- Developing new avenues via which businesses may find, recruit, and hire new personnel.
- Increasing the number of social relationships between individuals and groups.
- Creating new jobs in the social media and consulting industries.
- Providing a forum for group conversation and the exchange of ideas.

What is Facebook?

Facebook is a social networking service that allows users to connect with their friends, family, coworkers, other people, and groups of people who share the same interest. Users can send their friends photographs, videos, articles, and thoughts. Entrepreneurs must first understand how it differs from other social media platforms to get the most out of Facebook. When social media networks first launched, they concentrated on individual expression; however, Facebook promoted relationship development to foster an interconnected online community. Businesses can use social media to communicate with their consumers and target audience about changes in hours, sales and promotions, new product offerings, merchandise photos, and more. When you post new material, those who follow your Page get an instant notification and may share it with their network or a specific group of friends with just one click. Fans can leave comments and send you direct messages on your Page. Engaging with these followers and responding to their inquiries can turn a potential consumer into a devoted customer right away. Because their contacts can see which brands they follow, even followers of your brand who don't share your updates are public endorsers. Other networks, such as Twitter, which allows businesses to broadcast news or short written blurbs of up to 240 characters, may serve different objectives. Still, Facebook has created the most features of all the networks. This diversity exposes businesses to a large consumer base and allows them to engage with customers in various ways.

IMPORTANT POINT: The most crucial point is that Facebook was the first social media platform to attain long-term success. It exposes businesses to a broad and diverse audience while also providing a comprehensive set of features compared to other social media networks.

Chapter no.2.

Choose the right social platform.

First and foremost, recognize that just because a social network exists does not imply that you must use it. It would help if you first decided whether it makes sense for your company to have a presence on the platform, who uses it, and how they use it. Is it safe to assume that your target audience uses every social media channel available? The answer is almost certainly no. As a result, your brand should be present on the platform(s) that your customers use. It doesn't matter if you have great content and a very active Facebook presence if your buyer persona isn't there as well.

Let's take a deeper look at Facebook.

Facebook.

It's impossible to deny that Facebook remains the dominant social media platform. We shouldn't be surprised that keeping people on the site longer is a top concern, with over 2.5 billion active users. To help its users accomplish more on the site without leaving it, Facebook has introduced several new features in recent years. These include new Facebook Groups and live video streaming services, and an improved advertising platform (more on that later). I understand what you're thinking... "However, my company is unique, and these new services are ineffective for me." We wouldn't be able to sell ourselves on Facebook because our audience wouldn't be able to find our stuff there." Even if your target audience does not use Facebook for work, they are likely to utilize it for personal reasons – perhaps as a mental break from their workplace. In this regard, you might still be found and make an impression.

For instance, SurveyMonkey published an excellent Facebook post about using surveys to develop successful commercials, logos, and packaging using puppies (always a win in my eyes). It is to-the-point, eye-catching, and provides a consumer-friendly brand proposition.

Analyze your competitors.

Analyzing your competition is something you should do regularly in marketing, which is valid for social media. What social media channels do they use? What kind of information are they disseminating? How frequently do they share? Understanding your competitors' social media strategies and involvement might help you create a roadmap for what you should do as well. Even more crucial, studying your competition will help you identify ways to set yourself apart as a brand in the eyes of the target customers you're vying for.

Facebook was founded about a decade ago, but it has become considerably more visible and significant in most people's lives than anyone could have imagined. It has evolved into a more refined version of traditional word-of-mouth — and businesses are attempting to harness it as such. Here are five pointers to help you increase your Facebook influence.

1. Know your online presence.

Almost all organizations, charities, businesses, and people now have a social media channel (or they should be). To get the most out of your online presence, however, you must be able to answer three key questions:

- What is the status of my online presence? For example, we've had clients unaware of numerous Twitter, LinkedIn, and Facebook feeds and were sending out conflicting messages.
- Which social media sites are best for my fan/audience base? For example, Vine, a six-second video-sharing site, is ideal for the WWF's endangered species program, but not so much for the Samaritans' support work.

How are we gauging our internet clout? Are we tracking and evaluating where visitors go on our site, who retweets, and how many comments we get on our posts (and, more importantly, how many individuals have been fed this information?) Most platforms feature capabilities for tracking how many times your pages or articles have been viewed, how many clicks per minute you've received, what material is most famous (loved), and so on.

2. Recognize the most effective methods for influencing essential groups of people.

Once you've identified the most effective channel for reaching your intended audience, you'll need to choose the best strategy for influencing them via it. Should we create articles, films, or images, or should we use games, petitions, or other methods to engage our target audience? Keep them up to date on how many actions they've taken and how much time they've invested to date.

3. Produce shareable content. Make it easy to do so!

Facebook allows users to share material, making it simple to interact with campaign films, infographics, viral videos, posters, and other media in the most popular way possible. Because it's challenging to stand out on social media, you should spend all of your creative energies creating relevant photos to promote your posts and increase sharing chances. Make sure your material isn't too dense or lengthy and that people can comprehend and share it easily (and ownership). Why not compose a shareable chunk of text to accompany your postings - 140-character retweetable content?

4. Avoid starting and stopping your campaign.

When you first start on a channel, keep your audience involved by posting information frequently. Showcase previous projects and triumphs, the impact you've had so far, your 'storyboard,' or your personality - by communicating in this way, you'll generate engaged audiences. Keep your consumers and clients well-informed by staying on top of the information flow. However, do not bore them.

5. Finally, delegate the grunt work to someone else!

Relevant partners will gladly use your content, so keep this in mind as you create your campaign and adjust your plan. You may be a trusted partner in this initiative, and you could tap into networks that could immediately reach 1.5 million individuals, such as if you work with O2 Priority Moments. Suppose it can develop support and engagement in a meaningful and relevant way.

"Touch Yourself" for Breast Cancer Awareness is one of the best charities and environmental social campaigns from the previous year.

The Women's Health and Men's Health magazines started a campaign in October 2012 to promote early cancer identification through self-checks for breast abnormalities. A Facebook app was built to encourage people to self-check and share a selection of 14 pre-written postcards with their friends. This is the king of campaigns, a fantastic illustration of using social channels; the primary channel was Facebook, with sharable material that engaged the target audience and ways to urge friends to do the same.

Chapter no.3.

A Positive Influence on Facebook.

Do you want people to know, like, and trust you on Facebook? Do you want to see more clients and sales as a result of your social media efforts? When you post on Facebook, one approach to assure both things are consciously making a positive influence. This tip outlines five crucial considerations to make while establishing a Facebook presence that will significantly impact your followers' influence. Whether it's your personal or professional profile, you never know who is reading it and making a decision about you — should they like you? Should they have faith in you? Should they learn more about you? Whether you like it or not, personal branding plays a huge role in social media. Someone forms an opinion of you in 5 seconds, whether favorable, harmful, or neutral. Everything you say, do, write, and be on social media leaves an impression on someone else.

Here are five strategies to have a more positive impact on your Facebook followers:

1. Use a Professional Profile Photo.

Check to see that you have a professional picture of yourself on all of your social media profiles, not just a vacation selfie. Your photo can be more casual on your profile, but on your Page, it should be more professional.

2. Be Aware of What You Post.

When it comes to having a favorable impact on others, it's not only about how you appear; it's also about what you publish. Because who you are has a direct effect on others, consider the following questions regarding your posting style:

- Is this a good or bad thing? I strongly advise you to focus on the positive aspects of your situation rather than slamming someone or something else to make your point. Before you speak out against someone or something, make sure you have your facts straight. A tale always has two sides to it. You can still express your concerns, but do it in a factual, non-biased manner rather than ranting and raving.
- Am I being encouraging or dismissive and critical?
- Am I making a complaint or offering a solution?
- Am I contributing to the terror mentality with this post, or am I a voice of reason?
- Is it a judgmental or an embracing attitude?

And if you like to post many political or debate-related things because you care about them, be passionate about them, but understand that you will not please everyone, and you must be OK with that. Be sure of what you believe in, and don't be afraid to speak up.

3. Embody a Positive Communication Style.

Your communication style has a significant and direct impact on the people you communicate with and your ability to influence them. Here are some points to remember when interacting with folks on Facebook:

- a. **Assist others**
    - i. Seek for chances to impart your wisdom and experience in your areas of expertise.
    - ii. Do not advertise. Simply be of assistance and share what you know constructively.
- b. **Show your support for others by liking, commenting on, and sharing the posts of your followers.**
    - i. Congratulate others on their accomplishments.
    - ii. Offer encouragement to your followers when they are in need.
    - iii. Refer others to those who need assistance in areas where you are unable to assist. Your thoughtfulness will not go unnoticed.

4. Choose Like-Minded Friends.

With so many bogus profiles and scammers lurking on Facebook these days, it's always a good idea to do some research before accepting a friend request. Only individuals that share their thoughts and honesty should be followed back. Make contact with other people who share the same hobby, philosophy, or ideology as you.

5. It's Not All About You.

Keep in mind because Facebook was created in the first place. It's not to make money or sell our stuff. It's to interact with others and form friendships and positive relationships. So, when you're on Facebook, express your gratitude, admiration, understanding, and compassion for others. This strategy will have a far more favorable impact on how people view you and your company. The more you concentrate on people, the more you will develop a "know, like, and trust" relationship with them, which will lead to increased company success through leads, sales, and recommendations.

Top 10 Ways to Influence Facebook.

People now can share and stay connected thanks to modern social media. In contrast to traditional media, where only a few celebrities had a large fan base, anyone may participate. In the previous ten years, Facebook has grown exponentially, changing how people 'connect.' Facebook created the stage for Twitter, Instagram, and Pinterest to emerge. It's no longer only about engaging with people on social media. It has evolved into a vast social platform for everything from shopping to cooking to marketing to dating to expressing political, social, and economic opinions.

Social media can make or shatter enterprises and even relationships. Social media has such a significant impact that it may be utilized for marketing, economic activity, and as a platform for expressing one's opinions. As a result, we must exert influence over current social media to get the most outcomes. According to the above figures, 23% of brand marketers develop tactics to influence social media, yet they still fail. About 15% of customers use social media to look for local companies. Is it possible for these figures to rise? Will brand marketers be able to succeed in their endeavors? We'll talk about how Facebook is effectively impacted and use the platform to engage with our target demographic even more.

1. Share What You Love or Provide Valuable Content for Audience on Facebook

You've spent hours writing a fantastic article and hundreds of revisions until the final product is complete. However, you still have a long way to go. You must market your material where the target audience is. Upload your work to the Internet. Yes, please click "share." The share button possesses magical abilities. It can disseminate your work to a much larger audience than your social media following. If the information is interesting, individuals will share it with their networks, reaching a larger audience. We can't make people share our content. It will be up to our work to speak for itself. As a result, the content must be relevant and meaningful. Always keep your intended audience in mind when sharing content. The content/brand must be disseminated in the appropriate social media network. According to a global analysis, Facebook accounts for 56 percent of content sharing mechanisms. Teenagers and children are the most active sharing groups.

Quick tips for getting your Facebook content 'shared':

1. Make your material user-friendly.

2. Create intriguing titles – Make use of keywords and clear, concise headlines.

3. Create numbered lists and "why" postings to pique the consumer's attention.

2. Use Social Pilot to Post Consistently.

Numerous social media platforms, such as Instagram, Facebook, LinkedIn, Google Plus, Twitter, and others, have saturated the social media landscape. Simply logging in and out may be a considerable undertaking. We sometimes miss out on vital networks when sharing content. Social Pilot is a fantastic tool that allows you to sync all of your social media accounts. Registering a Social

Pilot account and linking all of your social media accounts are the only steps required. After you've scheduled all of your media postings in advance, you may make a single post and submit it to many forums at once. Its personalized Facebook branding includes an expressive function that boosts your blog post's visibility on Facebook. "Published by your Brand name" can be substituted for "published by Social Pilot." This not only increases your fan base but also offers your company an authentic image. In the category of Internet and telecom/social networking, Social Pilot is ranked #692. You can keep track of your postings, manage several social media accounts, and schedule content for different time zones. When you post content at the right time, it has a much more significant impact. When you're out of fresh content ideas, Social Pilot comes to the rescue. It's a fantastic online tool for bloggers and content marketers looking to make an impression on their audience.

3. Focus on One Facebook Marketing Strategy.

It's fantastic to churn out posts and publish them on social media networks regularly. However, performing too many things at once may make you appear overly excited. Don't try to work in a vacuum. Understand what your target market wants, generate high-quality content, devise a marketing strategy, and go for it. Switching your marketing plan from one to the other is not a good idea. The phrase "Content is King" has been around for a long time. As a result, focus on your content. Add statistics, citations, photos, links, infographics, and other references to the information to make it more valuable.

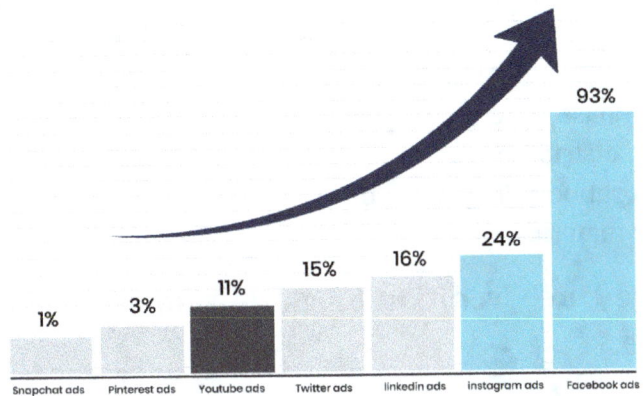

The following are the top three factors that make material effective:

- Relevance to the target audience (58%)
- Interesting and Compelling Storytelling (57 percent)
- Initiates a reaction/comment/discussion (54 percent)

To impact Facebook, focus on these three variables. Create a Facebook page strategy and only create material for related channels. As an influencer, you should understand precisely what your audience wants and craft your material so that it attracts attention.

4. Have a Strong Network Within Your Own Community.

Celebrities, authors, and other prominent figures respond to their Facebook fans in public. You can also offer personalized messages to your admirers to build a stronger bond with them. Create excellent Facebook posts to grow your fan base. Engage your audience and consider their comments. Incorporate their suggestions in appropriate spots. Produce better material in response to their expectations and requests. Your brand's best marketers will come from your fan base. Attempting to create a base in random locations may result in a dead-end. They'll distribute your content to others outside of your neighborhood. They'll be the most enthusiastic promoters of your material.

5. Give Due Credit and Acknowledgment to People.

Your target market adores you. They are eagerly anticipating your next launch or release. But do you give them the credit they deserve? A Facebook influencer will have an impact on his audience and remain in their minds. Always show your appreciation for their compliments. Earn your audience's trust by building a connection with them. As a brand promoter, you may use online competitions to pique the interest of your target audience. Give the prize recipients thoughtful and sincere presents. Conduct personal activities so that your fans form an eager network around you. Online behavioral tools are available that allow influencers to assess their audience's behavior.

6. Subscribe Feed of Top Blogs.

Even though the most important social media activity has nothing to do with you, if you're 'socially listening,' you might be able to alter the situation in your favor. One of the most aggressive blogging services is Tumblr. Enthusiasts from various walks of life gather to publish and share their works of art. You can follow and subscribe to any of these blogs based on your preferences.

The most popular blogs receive the most traffic, which allows for more comments, conversations, complaints, and ideas to be shared. And who knows, maybe you'll be the first to seize an opportunity! We've all heard the expression "right person, right location, right time." Some of the best internet marketing blogs don't simply focus on one topic; they cover a wide range of issues. If you subscribe to a high-quality blog like HubSpot, Blue Glass, or KISS metrics, you can significantly impact Facebook.

7. Persistence.

The Internet is inundated with an unfathomable amount of information. Furthermore, the human attention span is barely 8 seconds on the whole. As a consequence, "survival of the fittest" is the only option. As a brand/content marketer, it is your job to keep readers interested in your blogs and articles. Brands and marketing professionals must continually re-connect with their customers by creating a large amount of content. Of course, this information should be relevant to the fan base. Post your stuff. However, Facebook still has the upper hand in terms of numbers. It boasts 1.5 billion monthly members and is the most popular social networking website. So, keep posting till people are forced to pay attention!!

8. Participate in Local and National Events.

It's incredible to see how some people have thousands of Facebook fans. The potential of a person to influence an audience has expanded as social networks have grown stronger. As a result, if we become active players, we can significantly impact modern social media. SouthbayPavillion uses the concept of incorporating live tweets into events. It uses a unique and appealing writing style to become a Twitter 'trending topic.'

Contests and other social events can go viral if they are adequately publicized. Participate in online forums, discussion groups, and webinars. These occurrences could be pivotal in shifting your brand's dynamics. The goal is to get the attention of the proper people.

9. Be Updated, Savvy, and Use Word Terminologies# Hashtags, Emojis, and More#

Emojis were the most adorable thing ever invented on the Internet. These icons began to gain popularity among the online audience because they were amusing, vivid, and joyful. Recognized the popularity of emojis and created the hashtag emoji. Since the first #hashtag# was posted on Facebook, no discussion among teenagers, friends, or followers is complete without it.

Hashtag promotions by Red Bull and Coke were both exciting. These efforts were highly successful at influencing social media. On Facebook, people used the hashtag #Share a Coke to share their success tales. It was a craze that finally spread to everyone. #Hashtags, #emojis, and other internet acronyms (#hundreds of them#) are terrific ways to share incredible information that impacts modern social networking platforms like Facebook.

10. Be Authentic.

Earning the audience's esteem is the most acceptable approach to influence them. When it comes to social media sharing, be distinctive, creative, and different. Be yourself. Modern social media has become a far more significant part of our lives than we thought it would be at the beginning of the century. Incorporate images, videos, and other media into your material to keep readers engaged. You're on the right track if you produce engaging articles that are free of plagiarism and capture the attention of your readers. Your voice will be the one that sticks with your target audience.

Chapter no. 4

How to Grow Your Facebook Presence.

The Right Way to Grow Your Facebook Presence.

Having a strong, or even fantastic, Facebook presence may aid in your company's growth like wildflowers. But only after you've built a significant following and learned how to give them exactly what they want will this happen. Here are some excellent techniques for any business owner or marketer to boost their Facebook presence and help their company grow.

1. **Make a list of your goals and objectives.**

Identifying your goals and objectives is the first step in expanding your Facebook presence. It means that before you start blogging, be sure you know what you're pursuing. If you understand how each platform works, who your target audience is, and where they are located, you'll be well on your way to reaching your objectives.

2. **Make it clear that you are a human being.**

Give your viewers a glimpse of your human side. For this to work, you'll need to be active on social media often. Quite often, in fact! Please note that sharing a link is not the same as hoping that someone will read or click on your article. It entails showing up and communicating with everyone. Respond to your audience's posts and engage with them when they show interest. Show them who you are, and they'll want to read more of your articles or visit your website because they'll feel more connected to you.

3. Recognize Their Needs.

Understanding your audience's demands will enable you to communicate with them on a more personal level. Knowing what they like to read and what they believe in will help you figure out what you should present to them. Once you grasp this, you may provide them with everything they desire, including directing them to your website to learn more about your company.

4. Make the Icons Visible on Your Website.

Make sure to include the social media network emblems on your website. Those who read your work will have an easier time connecting with you if you do this. Make it easy for them to contact you rather than requiring them to search you down.

5. Connect Your Facebook Profile.

Connect your Facebook or other social media accounts to your profile. You'll want to link to your website from your profiles, just as you'll want to link to your website from your profiles so visitors can learn more about your firm.

6. Everyone should know about it.

Your Facebook accounts should be shared with everyone you know. Don't be spammy, but don't be scared to offer your information. They'll know you're on Facebook if you do this, and they'll be able to share your posts with their friends. It is an easy way to spread the word.

7. Develop a Facebook strategy that is integrated.

You should make sure that each social media network you use has a purpose. Starting a marketing calendar will help you do this. Make a calendar for all of your forthcoming events, blog entries, and whatever else you decide to do with your business. It will help you keep organized and understand how each of your social media profiles may assist your business reach new markets.

8. Produce High-Value Content

In some instances, you'll want to publish great content on your blog and social network sites simultaneously. Being able to attract and retain more customers and income is made possible by having the best content.

Everyone should be involved.

You want to interact with the people who leave comments on your Facebook sites. Meaning you should always reply to what other people have to say. Show them you're interested in what they have to say by letting them know you're listening and reading what they have to say. Then, offer them more of what they want to keep them posting on your sites.

9. Improve the performance of your Facebook accounts.

Using keywords to optimize your Facebook accounts is a must. Be specific about the terms you use. Put your consumers' search queries into consideration and include them in your postings.

10. Make use of hashtags.

Hashtags are popular these days. Everyone is utilizing them to increase the number of visitors who visit their sites or read their posts. Using hashtags on Facebook will help you attract more people to your social media accounts and website, but be careful how you use them. Don't end each post with 15 hashtags that aren't connected.

11. Include Social Media Icons in Your Emails.

Consider this: you send emails all day long. If you include social network symbols in your email, recipients are more likely to become inquisitive and visit your pages and, eventually, your website. This is a fantastic strategy to expand your social media following.

12. Provide a Benefit to Your Audience.

Your audience will appreciate it if you provide them with a benefit. 'What's in it for me?' say visitors to your social Facebook profile. Show them by giving something away for free - anything that will entice them to join your company by establishing a trust or pique their interest. Consider giving them a free trial, a free book, a discount voucher, or simply like back on their Page. This will assist you in gaining valued followers who will continue to engage with you.

13. Branch Out.

Use more than just Facebook, Twitter, Pinterest, Google+, and Instagram. There is a slew of different social networking platforms to choose from. This could include social bookmarking, social review, and other sites. You may also use Foursquare to update your location and let your customers know where you are. It's not only about the big guys when it comes to being social.

14. Use Games.

People enjoy responding to questions and being correct. Using trivia games to increase likes, followers, and traffic is an excellent approach to increase engagement and attract new consumers. It's also possible to have a lot of fun with it!

15. Post at a Comfortable Rate regularly.

It's aggravating to visit one of your favorite blogs and discover that it hasn't been updated in a long time. That implies that you should post frequently and at a comfortable rate. If necessary, you may always plan your postings ahead of time to avoid leaving your audience hanging.

16. Try Not to Outsource.

Attempt to post on your own Facebook accounts. It will give you a natural appearance. If you decide to outsource, make sure the person has a voice comparable to yours.

17. Do your research.

Each business will have a unique Facebook experience; for example, a restaurant will have a completely different strategy than a used car shop. Take the time to look into other methods for increasing the number of likes and followers on your social media profiles. Take a look around and learn everything you can about expanding your Facebook presence in your target market.

18. Give them a reason.

Give your customers a reason to like your Facebook page and follow you on the social media platform. Show them that you'll frequently be writing and that you'll be posting exciting updates. It will motivate them to interact with you.

19. Tackle Customer Complaints Efficiently.

If you receive a complaint through your Facebook page, respond quickly and effectively. Even if they aren't, respond and be professional. If you want to keep your customers happy, make sure you answer quickly to their inquiries. Providing top-notch customer support.

20. Provide Q & A's.

Use your Facebook page to ask and answer inquiries. Use a frequently asked questions area to respond to their questions quickly.

21. Ask Clients to Share and Connect.

You might be able to gain more followers simply by asking your clients and possibly even potential clients to share and interact with your Facebook profile.

22. Create a Plan and Stick to it.

Make a strategy to attract more admirers. Stick to your plan and do what you think will help you succeed more often. Stick with it if you find anything that works well.

23. Treat Each Social Network as an Individual One.

Treat each social media account separately. To attract more fans, share them individually and frequently.

24. Go Further in Customer Service.

Overcome obstacles to help others find a solution to their problems. That way, they'll know you're doing your best to help them out, and you'll be seen as a great person with a respectable company as a result. It will encourage them to return.

How to grow Facebook following in 2022: 9 essential steps.

How to Build a Facebook Fan Following

- Investigate your competition.
- Fill up your profiles completely (yes, your ones too)
- Maintain your brand's consistency.
- Distribute fantastic content
- Make connections with thought leaders and influencers in the industry.
- Make use of hashtags.
- Ads that you pay for should appear in your postings.
- Make eye contact with your audience.

I've become used to spending most of my waking hours on social media due to this. I still remember how happy I was when I initially opened a Facebook account and connected with people from my physical world. It seems stupid today, but it was a significant deal at the time. I eventually moved on to Twitter, Instagram, and LinkedIn, among other networks, since I needed to be on all of them. As I've gotten older and begun working in digital marketing, I've realized how important social media has become in everything we do as a society and how different life has evolved as a result. I'm using the majority of my free time on social media. I still remember how happy I was when I initially opened a Facebook account and connected with people from my physical world. It may seem minor to us now, but it was a big thing back then.

I eventually moved on to Twitter, Instagram, and LinkedIn, among other networks, since I needed to be on all of them. As I've gotten older and begun working in digital marketing, I've realized how important social media has become in everything we do as a society and how different life has evolved as a result. Through social media, brands are forming these same personal connections with their customers. You have more chances than ever before as a brand to communicate exciting news and insights about your company, build an online community of passionate individuals about your brand, and interact with customers on a more human and personal level than ever before. However, if you don't know where to begin, creating a following and connecting with your audience can be challenging for brands. This post will teach you the fundamentals of growing a Facebook following and the tools and methods that brands are employing to succeed on social media today.

- Fill up your profiles completely (yes, your ones too)

Now that you've decided where to create your profiles, it's time to get down to business.

Be precise and up-to-date.

Almost every social media network has a summary area, profile picture, and cover photo where you can enter and present information about your company; ensure sure this information is accurate and up-to-date across all platforms. There's nothing more perplexing than having one website address and another on your Facebook page. Establishing this general knowledge lends credibility and enables individuals to respond quickly if they so desire.

Creating profiles shouldn't be limited to company pages.

Each of your employees should have a complete profile, depending on the platform, so that they may offer corporate news, industry insights, and so on. Consider the increased reach you could achieve by implementing an employee advocacy campaign. All of their followers and connections will be exposed to your content as each employee acts as a brand ambassador for your company, sharing content on all of their channels. When creating these profiles, keep in mind that neither your company nor your profiles are ever fully complete. You should continually tweak and adjust things to improve the user experience and make your organization look good.

- **Maintain your brand's consistency.**

When I say consistent, I mean that the general tone of your social media presence should reflect your personality, values, and voice. Your written bio should be in sync with your profile photo, which should be in sync with your cover photo, which should be in sync with your content. Even more so, if you're using numerous social media sites, be sure that each account conveys the same story and has the same tone. Consumers want to connect with your business personally, and sending conflicting and contradictory messages will only confuse them and make them less inclined to stick around. In the end, whatever your company's tone is, stick to it. Building a social media following is heavily reliant on transparency and trust, which can be found in your profile and the content you post.

- **Distribute fantastic content.**

While creating material that your followers want to view and engage with is one of the most "no-brainer" ways to develop a following, it cannot be underestimated. Sharing high-quality content with your audience will help you establish your business — and your brand — as a thought leader in your field. Knowing what fantastic stuff is, it might be a struggle when it comes to sharing it.

What should you talk about?

Your stuff is the most obvious thing to share. On the other hand, many businesses develop exclusively distributing their material, which might backfire long-term.

Don't be a snob about content.

You're not doing it right if you're simply sharing your content. 70% of the time, the content you share should give value and enhance your brand; 20% of the time, it should be other people's articles and ideas; and 10% of the time, it should advertise yourself or your business. On Facebook, only 10% of your material should be self-promotional. Why? Because this allows you to gain followers' trust and give them valuable content and information. Would you stick with a company that solely sends you promotional offers? Most likely not. Apart from that, here are some suggestions on what to post.

Make your material more visual.

To make your postings more appealing, use visual content like photographs, gifs, and videos. Consider the expression "showing vs. telling." People want to see more than simply text, and something visually appealing to catch their attention is required. Users on Facebook displayed a high level of interaction with visual content, both image and video:

Consider going live.

Use live video to connect with your audience in real-time. According to studies, consumers spend three times as much time watching live videos as they watch pre-recorded ones. Take advantage of this new trend and communicate directly with your audience! Above all, keep an eye on the platform and how your audience interacts with it. Consider each platform's strengths and expected behaviors. If you have real-time material, a medium like Facebook will be more beneficial than Instagram. Alternatively, if the same material is being shared across many platforms, be prepared to change accordingly. If a long-form LinkedIn status receives a lot of attention, but the identical post on Facebook does not, your followers are telling you that they aren't interested in that type of content on Facebook, and you need to make a change.

- **When is it OK to share content?**

When it comes to knowing while to post on Facebook, it all depends on your audience. However, there are some guidelines you can follow when you're first getting started. Create a Facebook sharing schedule to discover when your posts get the most attention. To reach your target audience, you can work to choose the perfect day, time, and type of content to share. The more they interact with your postings, the more likely they will see your content in other news feeds.

- **Make connections with thought leaders and influencers in the industry**

As I briefly discussed previously, connecting with industry influencers will be a terrific way to develop your social media strategy and grow a substantial social media following. These are the firms or individuals who are thought leaders in your sector, and your customers and target audience follow them. Make use of that resource! Share articles from industry professionals that you read or watch with your audience. Your audience is likely to be following or connecting with them as well. Are you a regular attendee of annual events or conferences? Find the speakers and make contact with them. Begin virtual chats with them regarding the event or message you're eager to learn from them. If the speaker interacts with you (which they should), you might be mentioned in a post shared with their followers. Alternatively, tag your favorite influencer in a post and invite your followers to share their favorite thought leaders. It will allow you to engage with your audience and have dialogues with them. Last year, Mari Smith, a prominent Facebook marketing influencer, spoke at IMPACT Live 2019 and was ecstatic to share her experience with her audience. She is an excellent example of a social media influencer that wants to interact and engage with her audience.

- **Use hashtags.**

You have excellent material and connect with your audience, but how can you make your posts more discoverable to new people?

Use relevant hashtags!

To refresh your memory, a hashtag (#) or pound symbol (*cough* Natalie Davis *cough*) is used on social media platforms to direct users to specific material. You may make your Facebook page more visible in search results by using hashtags. Users may directly follow these hashtags, or related posts can be found by searching for them. Hashtags first appeared on Twitter, but they have subsequently spread across all other sites.

I'm not sure which hashtags to use.

The key to using hashtags efficiently is to figure out which ones are most relevant and popular with your target audience. Work for a house building company, for example. You might consider utilizing the hashtag "#homeremodeling" because it is linked to what your audience is looking for and is likely to be consistent with the type of content you are and will be providing. It's vital to remember that your hashtags should and can alter depending on the material you're sharing. While you'll employ repeating hashtags in your material, mixing it up will help you reach bigger audiences who are still interested in your niche.

In my postings, where do I put hashtags?

What's the short answer? It's a difficult situation. There is no one-size-fits-all approach to employing hashtags, and it can vary depending on the platform you're using. Identifying your most desired hashtag and using it immediately in your post is a wise rule of thumb. Consider putting related or secondary hashtags at the bottom of the post, in a comment or thread, so they don't detract from your content but still do well in search results.

- **Profit from sponsored content and paid adverts.**

Now that you've got your social media platform up and running, it's time to take things a step further. Organic views will only go you so far, and obtaining them is becoming increasingly challenging. Why? Because the platforms are astute, they want you to pay to play to acquire social media affluence. On the other hand, using social media to advertise is one of the most cost-effective methods of reaching a new, targeted audience at a low cost.

Facebook advertising.

As you've learned, getting people to notice your great content is critical to growing a social media following. However, with Facebook's recent algorithm modifications, information shared by friends and family now takes precedence over brand pages. Oh no... How will I ever grow a Facebook following if folks aren't viewing my content? This is when Facebook marketing campaigns come in handy. Because of the large number of individuals who use Facebook and the sophisticated targeting capabilities you have at your disposal, Facebook advertising may be quite advantageous to your business. Suppose you're trying to attract them to like your Page or want to share a particular piece of information with them. In that case, you have a decent chance of doing so by using Facebook's ability to target exact characteristics beyond gender and region, such as life events, buying behaviors, and hobbies. There is, however, a correct and incorrect method to use Facebook advertising to generate results. Boosting your posts will merely increase the number of people who see them.

However, suppose you want to grow your audience and increase interaction. In that case, you'll need to undertake a lot more detailed and targeted advertising to ensure that the correct material reaches the right individuals. Ali Parmelee, IMPACT's paid media strategist, and Facebook expert, explained why Facebook advertisements are valuable in a conversation. To utilize Facebook advertising to increase your audience, you must do more than turn it on. However, Facebook advertising has a lot of potentials.

- **Make eye contact with your audience.**

It's easy to get caught up with the number of likes and followers on Facebook. However, once you've built your following, you'll need to communicate with them regularly to keep them interested. React to posts in which you've been mentioned, answer questions when they're asked, and respond to comments on your material. If you have a query about which you are unsure, tag those thought leaders and industry professionals to obtain their feedback. It's the nature of social media to be sociable!

On Facebook, people enjoy interacting with brands. The more you do it, the more likely people will follow you or wait for me. Some firms have even become well-known for their ability to engage with their fans and customers.

Let's create a social media empire together!

You're probably fairly stoked to establish your social media empire now that you have the technology and the know-how.

Chapter no.5

Successful Facebook Influencer.

Influencer marketing is effective. That's why it seems like everyone these days aspires to be a social media influencer. This marketing is becoming more popular as a legitimate and successful approach to advertising and keeping your audience engaged in generating revenue. Over 3.7 billion people utilize social media today, and the influencer marketing sector is worth $5 billion!

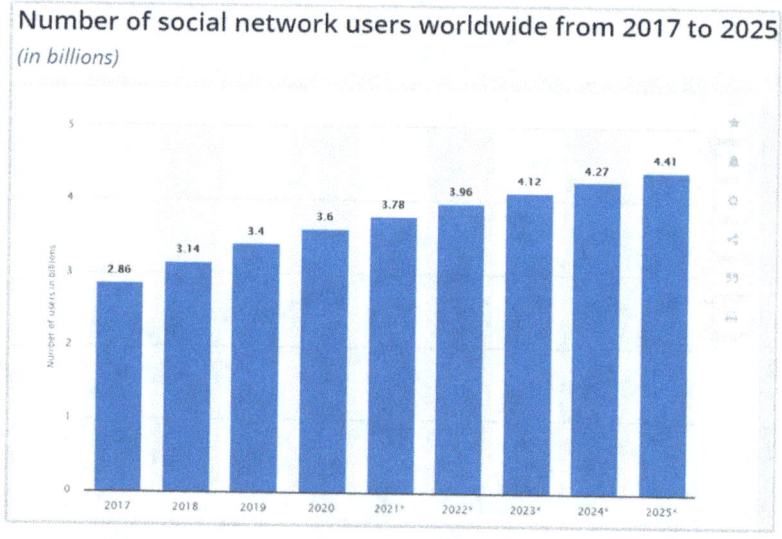

We need into consideration the fact that anybody may become a social media influencer (with the right approach), but it will take time and dedication to make this happen. For a reason, it's ranked as one of the most OK online jobs for college students, but keep in mind that it's not easy. Follow the steps to discover how to become a successful Facebook influencer.

How to Become a Facebook Influencer in 9 Easy Steps.

It takes patience and drives to become a Facebook influencer, and it will take at least a year of strenuous effort before you see any genuine benefits. Let's get right to the nine stages to become a Facebook influencer now that that's out of the way.

1. Pick a niche.

Picking a specialty is the first step in starting an online business. To build an audience of engaged individuals who care about your message, you must complete this step. Every marketing influencer you see on Facebook has a particular area of expertise. Without a distinct niche, no matter how many other advantages you have, you will have to fight with everyone else for your audience's attention. Furthermore, you will be speaking and marketing to everyone, which will result in you reaching no one. When deciding on a niche, consider the following questions:

- What are your passions?
- What do you excel at?
- What are your interests and passions?
- What are your hobbies and interests?
- Do you have any odd habits?
- What do you like to do?

For example, if you've always been into fitness and working out, becoming a social media influencer that encourages and motivates people to achieve their fitness objectives makes sense.

Any of these elements can become significant assets in assisting you in naturally attracting a group of people who share your interests. Make sure your pick matches your personality because that is the only way people will relate to and trust you. People can sense when you don't believe in what you're doing, and if you don't, they'll notice, and you'll lose your audience. However, when people see your genuine enthusiasm for the work you do, it becomes much easier to draw an audience and keep them engaged. Make sure your topic is something you enjoy, regardless of the niche you choose. It is critical to your long-term success because it will motivate you to keep trying when things become tough — even if it is just because you appreciate what you do.

2. Select your primary platform.

There are many channels you can use as a social media influencer, including:

- YouTube
- Instagram
- Twitter
- Tik-Tok, and more

It would help to establish your presence on the profiles you chose before beginning your campaign to become a

Facebook influencer. You can use a range of social media platforms, but you must pick one central platform to which you will devote the majority of your material. You can still be active and engaged on other social media platforms, but your focus will be on this one Facebook page. When it comes to choosing the ideal social media networks for you, there are numerous aspects to consider. To begin, find out which social media platforms other people in your field are using the most. Your niche will also determine your primary channel. Facebook may be the best option for some fashion influencers, whereas YouTube or Twitch may be the best option for video game influencers. Similarly, Pinterest, Snapchat, Twitter, and all other major social media networks may be more suited for different influencers depending on specific criteria.

- The audience you want to reach
- The critical channels used by other influencers in your area
- The type of content you'll create
- Your ease level in front of the camera
- Your ability to write interesting written content

In general, most influencers should start with Facebook because it has been there for a long time, may be lucrative, and has a well-established online presence.

3. Define your target market.

Aside from selecting the correct specialty, your success as a social media influencer is based on finding the right audience or community to support you. Your brand will be meaningless on social media if you don't have any followers, fans, or subscribers. So, before you start posting on Facebook, you need to figure out who your target audience is. You should concentrate on the people and communities who will provide the gasoline for your brand's success on Facebook. You'll probably discover your audience on Facebook if you're a lifestyle influencer. Here are the stages to defining your target audience:

1. Demographics.

To determine the ideal audience, ask questions like:

- What is the age and gender of my target audience?
- Do they have a home?
- Do they know how to use the Internet?

2. Challenges.

Ask and answer the following questions to learn more about your target audience's challenges:

- Are they familiar with your product or brand?
- If that's the case, why aren't they using your product?
- Or, instead, why aren't they using it as much as you'd like?

Consider all of the roadblocks that may have led up to this point.

3. Motivators.

Answer the following questions for the motivators of your target audience:

- In what ways may the people you're trying to reach be enticed by your brand or product?
- What is it about your product that entices them?

4. Pain Points.

Anything about your product or brand that can irritate the people you're trying to reach out to? Make a note of all the possible causes of your discomfort.

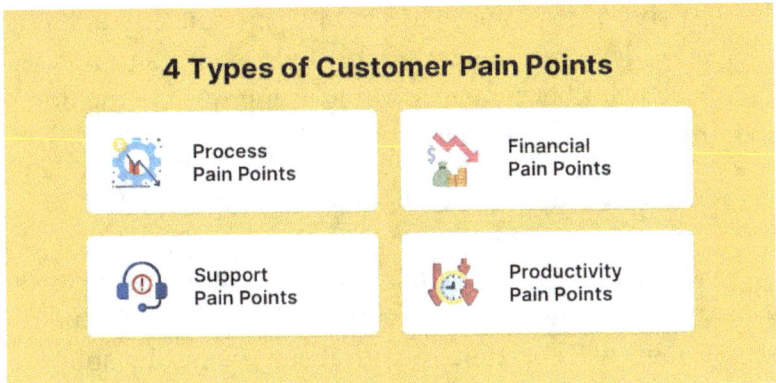

5. WIIFM (What's In It for me?).

This question is all about why your clients should use (or keep using) your products or services. You should be able to communicate the benefits they would receive clearly. By considering all of the characteristics above, you will zero in on your target audience on Facebook, where they are already active.

4. Develop a content calendar.

As a Facebook influencer, you must regularly provide great content that your audience (as well as search engines and social media algorithms) will appreciate. People admire social influencers who are dedicated and consistent. You must present a consistent message every day and create meaningful material relevant to your target audience. Once you've determined what kind of material you'll need, you'll need to construct a content schedule to keep you on track.

Some of the work for creating a content calendar will have already been completed in the preceding phase. Not only will completing the questions above help you identify your target demographic and where they're most likely to congregate on social media, but it will also help you choose the best sort of material to use in your influencer marketing campaign. Here are a few tips to help you plan out your Facebook influencer marketing approach, including creating a content calendar:

- Create and distribute high-quality content that is jam-packed with value.
- Plan your social media content marketing plan by identifying your objectives and the kind of material that will best help you reach them. Establish a posting schedule on the Facebook platform.
- Choose the periods when you're most likely to gain the most significant engagement from your audience when submitting your material.
- To construct your calendar, select the appropriate Facebook management tools. You can also make your own Excel calendar.
- Fill your calendar with a wide range of content formats, themes, and post types. Include information on the sites where the content will be posted, as well as times and dates.
- Finally, you have the option of scheduling your postings. It differs from constructing a content calendar. It entails using automated technologies like Buffer to set up a queue for your material to be uploaded on Facebook at predetermined times.

5. Strategically generate traffic.

The more Facebook traffic you can produce, the more influential you will become. Other individuals will follow you as your following grows, and you'll be able to use the power of social proof to reach an even larger audience of admirers and followers. However, you'll need to find strategies to intentionally attract traffic, in the beginning to get the ball rolling. Here are a few simple yet efficient methods for increasing Facebook traffic:

- Make it simple for your audience to share your material with their networks.
- To maximize your visibility, tag others and utilize the proper hashtags.
- Post your material when your target audience is most active.
- Interact with your audience regularly and deliver a lot of value.
- Invest in Facebook advertising to reach a larger audience.
- Make calls to action that are both innovative and persuasive.
- To increase your authority and reputation, network with other industry leaders.
- Establish positive media relations to increase media exposure and promotion.
- In emails, mention Facebook accounts in newsletters, welcome messages, outreach templates, and so on.
- To make your material stand out and maximize engagement and shares, include plenty of eye-catching visuals, such as photographs, videos, and infographics.

- Consider new ways to engage with your brands, such as presenting webinars, audio podcasts, video interviews, and more.

6. Collaborate with other influencers.

Collaborating with other niche influencers allows you to get fans from their followings. Working with Facebook influencers can help expose your material to a big new audience and bring even more traffic to your pages since their reach typically reaches millions. You can work with influencers in your field in a variety of ways. Paying people to promote your content or products is one option. However, when you are just starting, this might be difficult. Organically engaging with your audience may be the finest and most successful strategy to help you grow your following. To do so, simply request that they share your post whenever you publish something worth sharing. You may use this method to increase your chances of success by featuring influencers in your content by covering their tales, conducting interviews, or generating expert roundup pieces. Then, when you share the post, tag them, and the influencers will be more likely to share it with their networks.

7. Engage your audience

This is significant because if you don't engage with your Facebook audience regularly, they'll lose interest in your company and brand. Your content is crucial to your influencer marketing plan, but it won't matter how amazing or intelligent it is if no one engages with it.

Facebook and other social media sites want to see people interact with your content. It sends them a strong signal that you're sharing items that your audience wants to view, which provides the essential social proof for your content and social media actions (such as promotion and advertising). As a result, each social media site's algorithm will show your material to more people interested in the same topic. It's like a snowball effect: the more people who view your material, the more people see your content, which helps you generate even more interaction, and so on. Brands searching for influencers to help them with their social influencer marketing efforts also want people to encourage their followers to buy something (or follow the company) rather than merely watch the promoted content. In this type of effect, your audience must believe they know you personally as an influencer. You must express your gratitude to them and thank your followers for their support at all times.

8. Make it simple for companies to reach you

Another helpful strategy for growth as a Facebook influencer is to make it simple for marketers to identify and contact you. There's money to be made in every business and on every social media channel - but only if brands can discover you. Influencers are found on Facebook in a variety of ways by different brands. Alternatively, users might use the platform to search for relevant hashtags and determine which accounts have the highest interaction rates. Assuring that your contact information is clear and prominent will make it easier for marketers to contact you. Write a captivating bio that informs brands that you are an influencer who is open to working with them. If potential clients have to look for ways to contact you, they're more likely to give up and seek out another influencer.

9. Over-deliver on brand partnerships.

Always go above and above when working with brands to attract future bookings from that brand. Brands prefer to work with Facebook influencers that provide a lot of value, and any time you go above and beyond with your brand partnerships, you increase the chances of them wanting to work with you again. This is a great strategy that utilizes the tremendous law of reciprocity to your advantage. When you add value to a brand, they feel obliged to reciprocate by doing something for you. When dealing with your audience, this strategy also works well. Although you may encounter skeptics who believe you are merely providing excellent material in exchange for something in return, if you are consistent and sincere in your aims, your audience will eventually trust and appreciate that you are genuinely thinking about them. If you ask for anything from them (like their email address), they will feel forced to provide it to you.

It takes time and works to become a Facebook influencer. You'll be well on your way to establishing an enormous audience of interested fans and followers for life if you follow the steps suggested in this chapter:

1. Pick a niche.
2. Select your primary platform.
3. Define your target market.
4. Make a content schedule.
5. Collaborate with other influencers to strategically create traffic
6. Bring your audience into the conversation.
7. Make it simple for brands to get in touch with you.
8. When it comes to brand relationships, go above and above.

How to use Facebook analytics to assess the success of your approach.

This is not a set-it-and-forget-it situation: successful Facebook marketing necessitates ongoing maintenance. It's critical to keep track of and measure what worked and what didn't to figure out what worked and what didn't. That way, you may constantly improve your plan by learning, tweaking, and trying again. Facebook Insights, which measures data such as..., can be used to track audience interaction directly reach (the number of individuals who saw your posts) engagement (how many people liked, clicked, shared, or commented on your content). Which of your postings causes people to dislike your Page? In addition, Facebook Insights can help you determine which sorts of posts are most beneficial for your Page, so you can see whether your current content mix is working well for you. Check out our beginner's introduction to Facebook Analytics for more information. External technologies such as Google Analytics, Hootsuite Impact, UTM parameters, and Hootsuite Insights measure actions outside of Facebook, such as purchases or other website conversions.

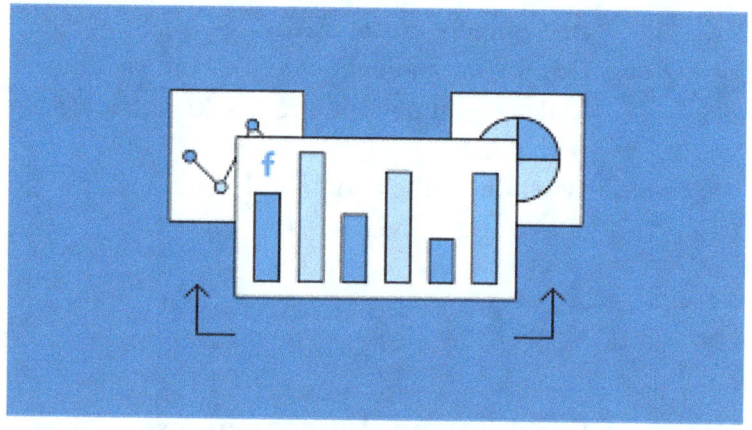

All of this to say, don't be intimidated! We've put together a step-by-step guide to help you track the return on investment of your Facebook marketing efforts. Not only should you celebrate and commemorate your successes, but you should also keep track of your progress over time. As well as tracking what's not functioning, keeping an eye out for changes is essential. Data will reveal what you should maintain doing and which strategies you should change. Over time, you may enhance your performance by defining goals, measuring results, and changing your plan in a continuous cycle.

Whew!

We understand that there is a lot to learn about Facebook marketing. However, the good news is that you may get started without spending any money. So, get your hands filthy and learn by doing. When you're ready, you'll get access to more advanced techniques and campaigns, as well as a wealth of resources and tutorials to help you along the way. Hootsuite can help you manage your Facebook presence as well as your other social media channels. You can plan posts, share videos, engage with the audience, and track the results of your efforts all from a single dashboard.

Chapter no.6

Use Facebook's Influencer Marketing to Your Advantage.

In January, Facebook revealed that its newest algorithm upgrade would de-emphasize business page posts in users' News Feeds. Many social media marketers were concerned at the time of the announcement that companies' organic reach, which previous algorithm adjustments had already hampered, would become a thing of the past on Facebook.

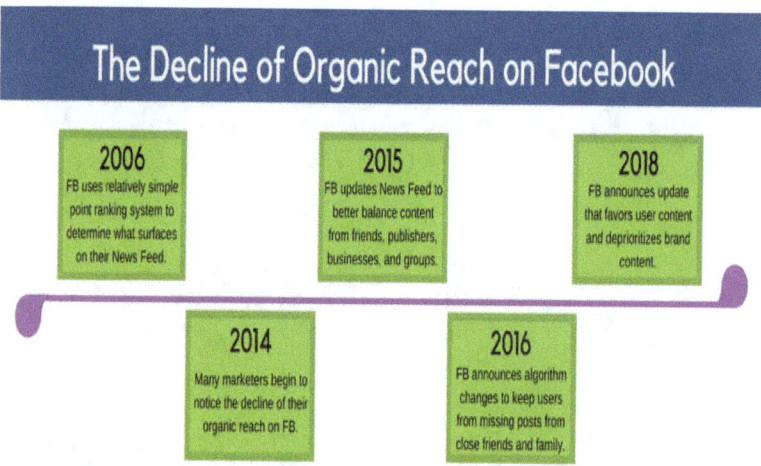

The most recent News Feed algorithm tweak indicates a future where Facebook is viewed as a pay-to-play advertising platform by businesses of all sizes. While "free" Facebook marketing options are securely nailed to their graves, marketers are becoming creative and seeking more genuine methods to connect with their audiences on social networking sites. Influencer marketing, which entails collaborating with influential social media users, is proving to be a promising tactic. To assist influencer marketing, Facebook has already launched a variety of tools:

- Since 2016, influencers have been able to properly designate posts that they've made in collaboration with a company using Branded Content tags. It keeps both influencers and brands in line with the FTC's sponsored content requirements.
- Facebook Groups for Pages allows businesses to build groups that are connected to their Facebook page. These Groups allow marketers to engage with their audience naturally (for example, Instant Pot uses their Group as a recipe-sharing space).
- A new boost function allows marketers to pay to boost the reach of a post made for them by an influencer. Brands can target a specific audience, and the post will appear to come from the influencer rather than the company. Before boosting an influencer's post, marketers had to share it through a brand's account.

How Does Facebook Influencer Marketing Work?

Influencer marketing on Facebook operates on the same principles as influencer marketing on any other online platform. It begins with a brand identifying a Facebook user with a medium-to-large (and highly-engaged) following similar to the brand's target demographic. The brand then contacts the influential Facebook user to see if they'd want to promote the brand's items on their Page.

Influencers expect to be compensated, so businesses new to influencer marketing should keep that in mind. While some micro-influencers will provide sponsored content in exchange for complimentary products, most influencers will charge a fee. After discussing the relationship, brands and influencers may negotiate compensation.

The influencer will create a certain amount of Facebook posts about the brand's product once the brand and the influencer have struck an agreement. They might post a video of the product being unboxed or a photo of themselves using it. Because the content comes from an influencer rather than a brand, it has a better chance of being seen by people interested in the product. And the target audience is more inclined to believe in a product recommendation from an influencer than in the brand's own words. Eighty-five percent of consumers say they trust internet evaluations just as much as personal recommendations. Isn't Facebook influencer marketing starting to sound appealing? Here's how to get started with your influencer marketing campaigns on Facebook.

Finding Influencers on Facebook

To locate influencers on Facebook, you have two options: manually scanning your existing Facebook fan base or using tools that will search the entire network for you. If you choose the manual search method, you'll need to find a group of Facebook users who have already expressed interest in your brand, possibly by sharing or commenting on your posts. You'll need to vet these potential influencers yourself after identifying them by looking at their social media profiles. Is their fan following large enough to make a possible collaboration worthwhile? Do they present themselves on social media in a way that is consistent with your brand? If you answered yes, you may contact them personally to see if they'd like to collaborate with your company.

Manually identifying influencers is time-consuming and may not be appropriate for firms that don't already have an influential, engaged Facebook audience. Use influencer identification tools, which are essentially search databases of bloggers and social media influencers, as an alternative. There are many of these tools, ranging in price from free to thousands of dollars per month. Most of them provide a free trial, so you can see how they function before you commit.

Defining the Goals of Your Campaign.

You should be thinking about the goals of your influencer marketing campaign when you start looking for and reaching out to power users on Facebook. Be as precise as possible. Instead of just setting a goal to "raise brand exposure," you may aim to "obtain at least 15k impressions" on an influencer's post. You might also wish to create goals for:

- Social media participation (e., likes, shares, or comments)
- Website traffic (e.g., how many people were attracted to your site due to an influencer's post?)
- Conversions (e.g., how many purchases or sign-ups did the campaign generate?)
- The campaign's revenue

To adapt a campaign to your aims, you'll need to collaborate with your influencers. The type of material that an influencer creates should be directly related to your objectives. If you want to drive visitors to a specific marketing page on your website, for example, the influencer must include a link to that Page in their post.

Ideas for Influencer Marketing on Facebook.

Influencers have a lot of freedom regarding the types of posts they can make on Facebook. Consider the following influencer marketing concepts.

Videos.

The video makes up over a third of all online activity, with 45 percent of internet users spending more than an hour viewing Facebook or YouTube videos every week. With the rise in video consumption, it makes sense for influencers to employ native Facebook videos to pique their followers' interests and drive engagement.

Facebook live:

Facebook Live is a live broadcast on Facebook. Facebook Live is still a relatively new format, but it allows companies and influencers to generate video content that seems true and in the moment. An influencer may stream themselves trying out your brand's goods or attend a live event sponsored by your company via Facebook Live.

Contests:

Offering prizes for participation in contests is an excellent method to increase your social media following and drive more traffic to your website. An influencer may share photographs of a product you're giving away, along with a link to your website's contest page.

Cross-Promotions:

Most social media influencers are active on many platforms and would like to run a campaign across multiple platforms. An influencer might, for example, create a blog post on a product or utilize a food brand's ingredient in a recipe on their website, then share the link on Facebook and other social media channels. Using as many channels as possible, you may reach a targeted audience.

Chapter no.7

Ideas for Facebook Influencer Marketing.

You understand how critical it is to establish a Facebook influencer marketing strategy. You also know how to discover influencers with whom to collaborate. Let's look at some of the most effective strategies for establishing a Facebook influencer marketing campaign.

1. Promoting Giveaway Contests

When looking for giveaway influencers, Facebook is an excellent place to start. It's possible that the goal of your Facebook influencer marketing strategy is to increase brand awareness and engagement. In this example, you could create a contest that the influencer could conduct on their blog or host it on your website. The influencers will then share a link to the contest page on Facebook to promote it. Because there's something in it for them, giveaway contests are an excellent method to engage a new audience. They'll eagerly engage with your brand if there's a chance they'll gain something valuable from it.

For their Unstoppable Women campaign, Ziera Footwear nails this strategy by merging it with cause marketing. The brand executed a giveaway campaign with key fashion influencers like Stylendipity's Katherine Saab. The contest was hosted on the blogger's blog, and she then marketed it on her Facebook page. You can also use Viper to host your giveaway. For a chance to win prizes, the influencer might urge their followers to like, follow, or comment on their posts. Customers who buy or refer their friends can also be rewarded through the platform. They can earn points for each purchase and use them for a reward later. If you're ready to launch a product or an app, Viper is also an excellent option. The Facebook influencer will create excitement about the launch and persuade their followers to sign up for a waitlist even before you launch.

2. Using Facebook Ads to Expand the Audience

for Influencer Campaigns.

Increase reach by using Facebook advertisements to promote branded content shared by the influencer. You can't ensure that all will see every piece of the material posted by a Facebook influencer of their followers. It's challenging to reach your target audience organically due to an overabundance of feeds and an ever-changing algorithm. You may target your preferred audience, optimize for your specific aim, and obtain campaign information by boosting influencer content using Facebook advertisements. You can automate the entire procedure if you use a service like Sendinblue. Create customized advertising, identify a target demographic, configure settings, and access data using the sales and marketing toolkit. Using the platform to launch an influencer ad can help you reach a larger audience. Sendinblue lets you be where your consumers are, whether it's on Facebook, email, SMS, or chat. From your CRM, you can trace every customer interaction and develop partnerships.

3. Sharing Experiences through Facebook Live.

You've probably heard that Facebook videos are a popular type of content. The platform's live video, though, is even more captivating. According to Facebook, consumers spend three times as much time watching live video feeds as they watch standard videos. So, if you want to use Facebook influencers to engage your target audience, have your influencers go live. Influencers can share their experiences with your business or product on Facebook Live. They may record themselves utilizing or attempting to use your goods for the first time. They might broadcast a live video of their visit to your store or perhaps a live event you've staged. Facebook Live can be used in a variety of ways in your Facebook influencer marketing strategy.

The Best Friends video game producers, for example, teamed with influential personalities like Laura Clery, who has over 3 million Facebook friends. Laura used live streams to interact with her fans and show them how to play the game. But she and her spouse also followed her standard plot by portraying Pamela and Roger, characters from her earlier videos. They were able to keep things lighthearted and entertaining while still advertising the game. To date, the video has gotten 9000 comments and 8,300 reactions. It's been shared over 800 times as well. It demonstrates that the influencer could effectively engage a large number of people via the Facebook Live broadcast.

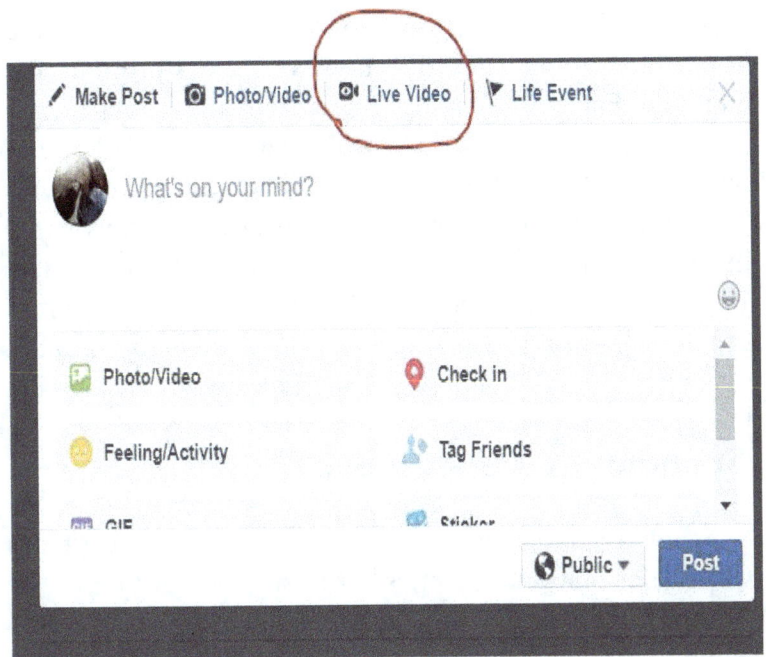

4. Cross-Promoting Campaign from Other Platforms.

Even if you've had success with influencer marketing on other platforms, Facebook allows you to increase the performance of your campaign even further. Perhaps you already have a campaign in a place where influencers write a blog post about your items. You can also ask them to promote the material on Facebook to increase its reach. This is how Minnie & Maxxie's influencers improved the brand's brand awareness campaign's performance. In a case study, Scrunch discovered that cross-promoting the campaign across many channels resulted in significant levels of engagement and exposure. Exclusive access to the brand's items had been granted to a select few fashion and style influencers. These

Instagram influencers helped spread the word about the new product range. They did, however, cross-promote the content on Facebook to increase reach and engagement. Here's an example of a post by When Words Fail's twin bloggers, Nicole and Danielle. The brand collaborated with 19 influencers, who each posted images of the firm's items with their Instagram and Facebook followers. The influencer material generated about 18,500 direct engagements during the campaign. The campaign was able to reach a total of 333,445, thanks to Facebook.

5. Standing Up for a Cause.

For a good reason, cause marketing is one of the most popular marketing tactics for businesses. A brand that stands up for a cause is a great approach to humanize it. It's a technique of demonstrating to your audience that you're concerned about specific concerns, whether they're social, political, or environmental. Including an influencer in your cause marketing effort improves its effectiveness even more. So, if you're planning a Facebook influencer marketing campaign, ask them to promote a cause that you believe in. Because he could play the part of an influencer, Joseph Gordon-Levitt found it easier to execute an influencer cause marketing campaign for his brand, Hit Record. Hit Record teamed up with Find Your Park, a non-profit organization dedicated to preserving America's national parks. By developing branded products, Hit Record aided the cause. The products were then promoted on Joseph Gordon-Facebook Levitt's Page. By doing so, he assists in promoting the cause while also presenting his company as a supporter of the cause.

6. Telling Stories Using Videos.

On Facebook, video content consumption is rising, making videos ideal for expressing your brand's narrative through influencers. According to TechCrunch, Facebook users watch an average of 8 million videos per day. People view 100 million hours of Facebook videos per day, according to Recode.

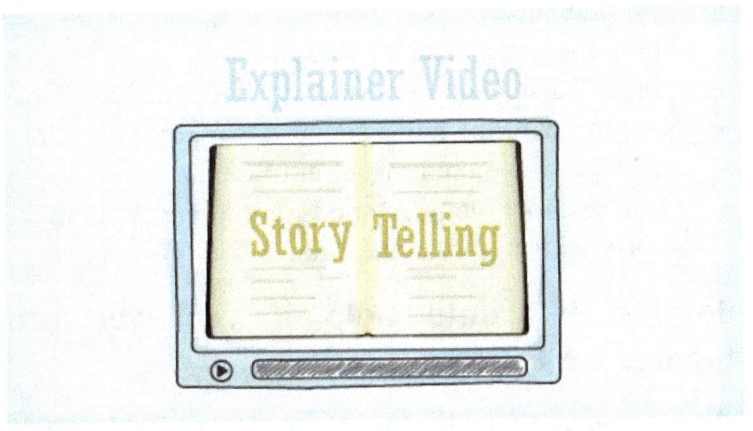

It demonstrates the importance of video content in engaging Facebook users. A great example is the Viral Nation case study of a Crayola influencer marketing effort. The campaign's purpose was to generate interest ahead of the new Crayola Air Marker Sprayer release. Crayola collaborated with social media influencers to create videos that told different stories. While some influencers developed films demonstrating how to use the product, others added a humorous spin to the content. For example, Your Everyday Canadian made an amusing video in which he uses the sprayer to earn money for pizza. This video has received approximately 800 reactions and has been viewed 577,000 times. In addition, the campaign resulted in 4 million engagements and 7.1 million impressions.

How do you become a Facebook influencer?

You may become a Facebook influencer by using the strategies listed below:

- Improve your Facebook page's optimization.
- Identify your area of expertise.
- Recognize who you're speaking to.
- Use intriguing and entertaining material to captivate your audience.
- Make a schedule and stick to it.
- Get your listeners interested in what you're saying.
- Keep up with the latest social media trends, such as hashtags, video, and Instagram Stories.
- Observe how your methods are doing and make adjustments based on the data.

Followers, it would help if you were an influencer on Facebook.

With so many variables to consider, there isn't a single figure that is the correct answer for every business. But you may categorize yourself as an influencer using specific broad characteristics. As an example, consider the following:

- Carrying less than 1,000 followers are nano-influencers.
- There are two types of
- influencers: micro (with less than 5,000 followers) and macro (with over 100,000).
- For example, well-known artists, singers, actors, and sports stars are examples of mega-influencers.

Ready to Get Started with Facebook

Influencer Marketing?

For a Facebook influencer marketing campaign, these are some of the finest strategies to work with influencers. You understand how to locate the ideal influencers to collaborate with and how the campaign will benefit you. All you have to do is start devising a strategy for building a profitable Facebook influencer marketing campaign.

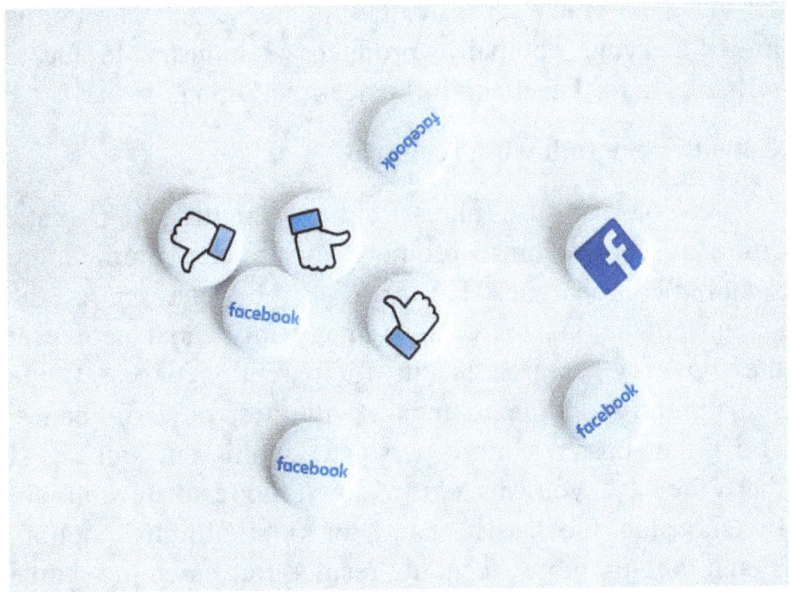

How to Find Facebook Influencers.

Now that you've learned about the advantages of Facebook influencer marketing, it's time to start looking for influencers to collaborate with on your project. However, discovering influencers on Facebook is more complex than other platforms because of content restrictions and privacy rules. So, what's the best course of action? To make your search easier and locate excellent Facebook influencers to collaborate with, follow these tips:

1. Keyword Research on Facebook.

If you're using Facebook to perform your search, you should seek pages rather than individual accounts. What is the reason for this? Everyone should quickly access the influencer's content for your campaign to have the most significant impact. And individual account privacy settings can make this difficult. Choose relevant terms linked to your company, product, or industry to locate influencers for Facebook influencer marketing.

Consider the following scenario:

You can use phrases like "parenting," "parent," "mother," and so on to promote your goods to influential social media parents. However, as you can see in the screenshot below, there aren't many influential people at the top of the search results for parenting pages. While some brands continue to engage with these powerful pages, you might prefer a more personal, one-on-one impact. If that's the case, you can narrow down the results even more by choosing the "artist, band, or public figure" option. You'll obtain more accurate results for parenting guide authors and parenting experts if you do this.

2. Four-star Media.

Another tool for finding Facebook influencers is Four-star Media. You can search for top Facebook influencers by filtering results by the platform on the platform. Narrow down your search by influencer reach, engagement rate, audience type, and influencer posting frequency to get a more refined list. In addition, the influencer platform provides you with influencer reports that reveal whether the influencer's material is relevant to your company. You may also compare Facebook influencers based on characteristics such as hashtag usage, likes, campaigns handled, and followers. With Four-star Media's unlimited influencer searches, you can narrow down your results to a Facebook influencer that has the correct following and is a good fit for your company. Their dashboard also includes campaign performance projections, such as estimated influencer media value and ROI estimates.

3. Sprout Social.

Use Sprout Social to manage your Facebook influencer efforts. You may use the site to find influencers in your field and contact them. You can keep track of what the campaign's Facebook influencers are up to, monitor specific hashtags, and keep an eye out for mentions. By adding individual campaign tags, Sprout Social allows you to track what the influencer shares. The tag report can then be used to see how well the campaign performs on Facebook. The number of messages sent, impressions, engagements, growth patterns, and clicks are among the statistics you'll receive. The Sprout Smart Inbox also makes it simple to observe people's discussions with various hashtags. Watch out for particular allusions, too. You can see how much money influencers make for a campaign by giving them affiliate codes or tracking links.

These are some of the most effective methods for locating Facebook influencers for your influencer marketing strategy. If conducting influencer research is too time-consuming for you, you can hire influencer marketing firms. These companies can connect you with some of the best and most relevant influencers for your business. They will conduct the necessary research and communication for you to run a successful campaign.

4. Using HYPR.

It can take a long time to look for Facebook influencers manually. But it's necessary if you're on a tight budget and can't afford to buy a tool. HYPR, on the other hand, is a beautiful alternative if you can afford to invest some money in effective influencer marketing techniques. The benefit of HYPR is that it doesn't only follow an influencer's Twitter data. It will also pull information about the influencer from other social media platforms, such as Facebook. As a result, you'll have no trouble finding relevant Facebook individuals with a lot of power on the platform. HYPR will display the number of Facebook followers the influencer has, as shown in the screenshot below. It will also display how many likes, comments, and shares they receive on the platform. The application also provides a demographic analysis of the influencer's audience. It makes it much easier to locate influencers who are relevant to your target market.

5. Insight pool.

Another excellent tool for spotting influencers across all social media channels is the Insight pool. You can locate Facebook influencers and obtain a thorough picture of their social media activity using this tool. It will allow you to narrow down influencers based on the type of material they make and share. The tool displays all of the themes in which the influencer specializes, as shown in the screenshot below. You'll also be able to see the businesses she's worked within the past and how she assisted with campaign execution. These are some of the most effective methods for locating Facebook influencers for your influencer marketing strategy. If conducting influencer research is too time-consuming for you, you can hire an influencer marketing service. These companies can connect you with some of the best and most relevant influencers for your business. They will conduct the necessary research and communication for you to run a successful campaign.

Conclusion:

Facebook has the most significant influence on customers of any social media network. In terms of influencing purchases, Facebook has outperformed other websites. (Image courtesy of The Manifest). According to a new study, Facebook users are more likely to buy from brands they follow than users on the other seven social networks evaluated. This is because social media has improved companies' ability to communicate with customers and vice versa. Because it is the most popular and successfully boosts brand recognition, Facebook is likely to be the most successful channel.

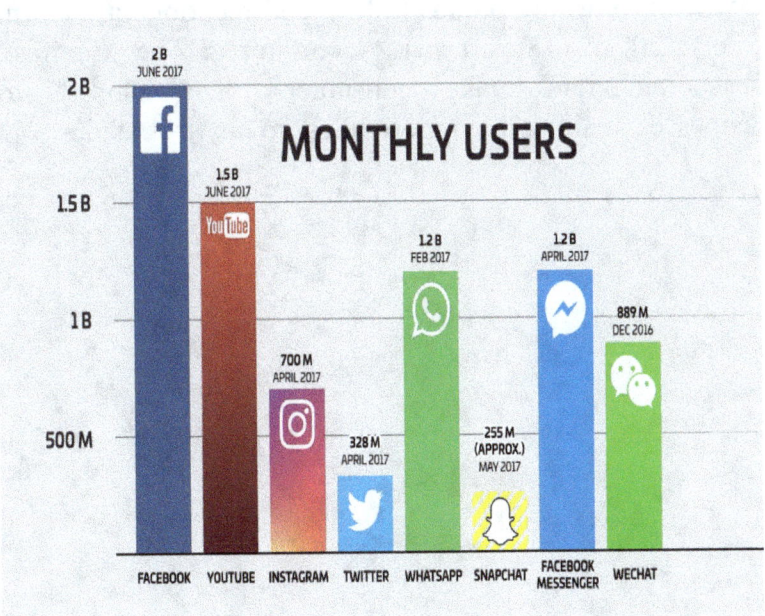

According to a new survey published by The Manifest, consumers choose to buy goods based on the companies they follow on Facebook rather than YouTube, Twitter, Snapchat, Reddit, Pinterest, LinkedIn, and Instagram combined. In this study, 52 percent of respondents (nearly 500 US social media users) said they bought something based on what they saw on Zuckerberg's platform, compared to 48 percent who said they purchased something based on what they saw on other sites. It is assumed to be due to Facebook's well-established social networking status. Multiple generations have used it, and its targeting algorithms do not appear to have harmed the situation. In general, social media can connect users and brands. Individuals increasingly appear to interact with corporate structures in a variety of ways. They include, according to reports, liking branded postings (51%), referring brand names on personal profiles (22%), sending private messages to brands (20%), and mentioning them in tweets (20%). (18 percent). According to The Manifest, these behaviors make consumers "feel closer" to businesses, making them more likely to buy from them.

This book is part of an ongoing collection called "Social Media Influence."

1. Increasing your Social Media Influence on Facebook.
2. Increasing your Social Media Influence on YouTube.
3. Increasing your Social Media Influence on WhatsApp.
4. Increasing your Social Media Influence on Instagram.
5. Increasing your Social Media Influence on TikTok.
6. Increasing your Social Media Influence on Snap Chat.
7. Increasing your Social Media Influence on Reddit.
8. Increasing your Social Media Influence on Pinterest.
9. Increasing your Social Media Influence on Twitter.
10. Increasing your Social Media Influence on LinkedIn.

Please check out Amazon for more books in this collection.

Author Bio

Aaron Cockman. Aaron enjoys reading and learning more about being profitable on social media, so she decided to write about something she is passionate about. More books will come in this collection, so follow her on Amazon for more books.

Thank you for your purchase of this book.

I honestly do appreciate it and appreciate you, my excellent customer.

God Bless You.

Sherry Lee.